BREATHE

IT'S NOT PERSONAL. IT'S PURPOSE

A STRATEGY THAT WILL TEACH YOU HOW
TO BREATHE THROUGH LIFE'S CURVEBALLS.

SHALYN GENOBIA WHITE

IT'S NOT PERSONAL IT'S PURPOSE

Breathe. It's Not Personal. It's Purpose. Shalyn Genobia White
Copyright © 2018 Shalyn Genobia White
All rights reserved.

Although the author have made every effort to ensure that the information in this book was correct at press time, the author does not assume and hereby disclaim any liability to any party for any loss, damage, or disruption caused by errors or omissions, whether such errors or omissions result from negligence, accident, or any other cause.

This book is not intended as a substitute for medical advice of physicians. The reader should regularly consult a physician in matters relating to his/her health and particularly with respect to any symptoms that may require diagnosis or medical attention.

No parts of this book may be reproduced in any form or by any electronic or mechanical means, including information storage a retrieval systems, without written permission from the author, except in the case of a reviewer, who may quote brief passages embodied in critical articles or in a review.

All scripture references used in this book were taken from the Holy Bible, Common English Version and can be found at: http://thebiblegateway.com.

Formatting and Design: Sidjae Price, Ph.D. | www.sidjaeprice.com
Editor: Godwin Tiewah | faithsworth@gmail.com

Printed in the United States

IT'S NOT PERSONAL IT'S PURPOSE

DEDICATION

I dedicate this book to God and myself. Lord, without you, I am nothing, and I can accomplish nothing! Thank you for the struggle, thank you for the silence, thank you for loving me enough to tear my world to pieces, and loving me enough to put me back together again gracefully, whole, nothing missing and nothing lacking. I thank you. To me, happy 30th birthday, you did it, Shay! June 14th, Gemini gang.

IT'S NOT PERSONAL IT'S PURPOSE

CONTENTS

Introduction 1

A Love Letter from Pain 5

It's Not Personal, it's Purpose--Romans 12:1-2 7

Silence 8

Afraid of Silence 19

Sharing is NOT always caring! 29

A Love Letter to Pain 32

It's Not Personal, it's Purpose--Romans 8:30-31 33

The Calling 34

The Gift 43

It's Not Personal, it's Purpose--Psalms 25:8-12 47

Identifying my Gift 48

Tired of Crying 51

It's Not Personal, it's Purpose--James 1:2-4 52

Trust the Process 53

It's Not Personal, it's Purpose--Psalms 32:8 63

Breathe 64

It's Not Personal, it's Purpose--Jeremiah 29:11 66

It's Not Personal, it's Purpose--Prayer 67

IT'S NOT PERSONAL IT'S PURPOSE

INTRODUCTION

Have you ever battled with stress, anxiety, depression, fear, loneliness? Do you ever feel like deep inside, your soul is screaming so loud that you're afraid someone will hear you? Have you ever cried until you lay breathless on the floor? Have you ever pleaded out for help or a strategy and everyone either turned their backs on you or simply just didn't know how to help you! Have you struggled with faith, hope, positivity, love, patience? Then this one's for YOU! I know exactly how you feel!

In chapter (age) 28 of my life, I had reached a place of misery, unhappiness, loneliness, and dissatisfaction with who I thought I had become at that time and where I felt I should already have reached by that stage of my life. I had rekindled a relationship, I thought I had cut off all negative ties before this point, yet I was unhappy! Though I had my own "life" occurring at the time, I use to spend my extra time focused on the outside world and its opinion and viewpoints. Eventually, the outside world consumed and contaminated my life.

All my choices and decisions were based on other people's opinions and views. During this process, I really lost sight of who I was. It didn't help when everyone around me seemed to be progressing along in this thing called life. I'm seeing engagements left and right, baecations, weddings, houses being bought, businesses being started, and money being "secured". Everyone seems to have it figured out!

Everyone is soaring and flying by, and then there's me. Constantly "TALKING" about how others got it figured out and drawing all kinds of conclusions; instead of trying to figure out where it is that I've been going wrong and how I can get it right! Throughout chapter 28, I did a lot of research. I investigated my family, my friends, my relationships, my actions. I told myself at chapter 29 I was going to make some "grown-up" decisions because I refused to experience another year of the same cycle.

Therefore, chapter 29 arrives, and I remain true to myself and keep my word! I made the decision to let go and cut off everyone and everything that was attached to me! I had personally reached a place mentally where I felt like I could not figure out my next move. Hell, I was fed up and tired of trying to figure everything out! I had made the conscious decision to quit my 9 to 5 position as a supervisor at UPS and focus solely on walking my own path and figuring out who I am and what I should be doing. This decision was nerve-wracking, yet very liberating to feel "in-control"

... HA! HA! HA! YEAH RIGHT!!

Therefore, chapter 29 is all about Jesus and me! After nearly dying and battling demons, (we'll discuss this later within the book) that I have exerted all physical and possible avenues. It's "either" you or I Jesus!! Let's just say chapter 29 has been nothing short of painful, long, and scary.

OHHHH, WHAT.... you thought I was going to promise you rainbows and unicorns, right?? NAH!

Along with that, it was interesting, promising, peaceful, fulfilling, powerful, liberating and freeing! YES! I gave up a lot and lost a lot! However, I've gained so much insight, value, self-worth, love, clarity, and contentment on WHO I am and most importantly, WHOSE I am! I've had the opportunity to think clearly for myself, create a plan and strategy for myself and execute goals along the way! I've learned what makes me tick, what I'm patient for, the type of energy that I will allow into my space, the words that I will allow to be spoken into me.

Chapter 29 has ripped me to pieces, as God placed his love and grace around me and put me back together again...WHOLE; Nothing missing, nothing lacking. As I am writing this book I am just days away from chapter 30, I am now more in tune with myself. I now have a clearer understanding of my purpose and my calling. I've had the opportunity to put my own life under a microscope and dissect me.

All of this had to take place within this silent space of my life! I had to spend alone time with me, I had to go through the pain, I had to scream and cry, I had to reach that dark space in my life. I had to hit rock bottom or ground zero! It's painful, it's scary, but it is attainable, and it's so liberating to live purposely and purpose-filled! Therefore, to anyone who may be offended or confused at this new level that I have reached, just know...

It's not personal, it's purpose!

A LOVE LETTER FROM PAIN

Can you hear that? My heart is banging against my chest, and my soul is screaming. My hands tremble as sweat secretes through to the tips of my toes. Rivers flow from my eyes as mucus meets my cheeks. The voices have grown into conversations, and those too have turned into screams. Do you see me? I know you're looking at me, but do you SEE me?

"Bruh", "Sis", "Chile"

This is what we say when we tag each other all day long on social media. We tag each other in silly relatable memes, and viral videos. However, do you see me?
I shared my sexiest video, I took a moment to prime my face and popped a little shimmer on my lips, and I even arched and darken my brows. You could comment and call me gorgeous, beautiful, a queen, but do you see me?

You mention how you've been watching my grind and respect my hustle, and how it seems I got it all together! You congratulate me and tell me you're so proud of me. Share with me, how you saw my potential in the past. However, how can you be proud of, what I can merely even grasp? You stand on the opposite side of my line of vision, and still I ask... do you see me?

Remember it's Not Personal, it's Purpose!

ROMANS 12: 1-2

So, brothers and sisters, because of God's mercies, I encourage you to present your bodies as a living sacrifice that is holy and pleasing to God. This is your appropriate priestly service. Do not be conformed to the patterns of this world but be transformed by the renewing of your minds so that you can figure out what is God's will. What is right, pleasing and mature.

SILENCE

It is amid your silence that you tend to hear the most, at least that what's everyone says. It took me the longest time to be comfortable in a tranquil state. We all have our quiet moments and a little hour here and there to ourselves, but silence is indeed golden. Amid my silence, is when I hear myself the loudest. In the core of my silence is when I become in tune with myself the most, this is when I get to dissect my emotions and get to feel the pain, pleasure or happiness that I am experiencing at its crest.

It is within that silence that I get to dissect who I am, I get to put my life under a microscope, and I get to focus on just breathing. I get the opportunity to take that in, appreciate each breath for what it is…, and dissect me. Within my silence, that's when I get to understand whether I am, who I think I am. Whether I can do what I think I can do, or whether I want to even to do it. What I think, I can do!

Its only within my silence I genuinely get to soul search and fully understand, and feel what's making me happy, what's making me sad, am I building to become a better individual, a better human being, am I doing everything that I was purposed for, everything that I was created for.

When you take a moment just to be silent and literally hear nothing physically around you, you get a moment to dissect your life. You really get to think about your impact and, the people who you inspire. Whether they make you feel a specific type of way or if you may be influencing them. You get to take time to think about what you're good at, whether it flows from a genuine, authentic place.

You get time to reflect on who you are as an individual, not as that woman, not as that man, but just as a living vessel. We all have a purpose, and we all are out here, trying to soul search and figure out our way. The truth is the more in tune we become with ourselves, the more we begin to understand our purpose and who we are. We realize that we are more than just the title of our name that we are more than just a being, that we are living pre-ordained spectrums

We all have our color to add to the frequency, we all have a reason to radiate, we all have a right to speak, to breathe, to co-exist amongst each other.

You just must try to understand what your purpose is and who you are!

Some years ago, I met a woman who was a "prophet" at a friend's church. I remember her speaking life within me within our brief encounter. I had to be about 20 years old. Around that time, I had been going through and dealing with a few things that I knew I didn't deserve and was not a part of my Karma! Earlier that week I had prayed about it and didn't give it much thought afterward. Her exact words to me were,

"Baby, I know you keep wondering why God has allowed what he must to take place in your life, and how you feel that some of the things that you are experiencing in your life are unfair. I just want you to know that it's not necessarily that you have done anything wrong, don't look at it like that. It's about the people that God wants to reach through you! Your story is going to help and release other women who are going through what you have and will be delivered and set free because of your story and your purpose".

It was so strange to me, because the moment that I had just had with God before this encounter, crying, praying, and asking, "Lord, why me"! He spoke to me through her, he confirmed me! In addition, for 9 years her voice has resonated inside of me! I tend to remind myself of that little gem from time to time when the going gets a little rough!

I always wondered what exactly was it that she meant by my story would help someone else. Why did God see it fit me to have to go through all the hell that I have just to help someone else? Just to be a blessing to someone else? Yes, I enjoy people so much, and I am such a social person, and I want to help and give back, these are genuinely my hearts desires; but why the long-suffering just to help others? It wasn't until this moment that I saw and understood the reasons for my experience.

In the solitude of your silence, you start to see and understand just how cluttered and loud your world is. The more contaminated your space is, the less pure and unhealthy it is for you to process a single thought or endure an independent emotion properly. In your silence, you get to understand why things make you feel a certain way, your reactions to problems, and why you allow individuals to do and say as they please to you. You start to understand more about yourself, you take the time to try to understand why you may be feeling an emotion at a time. In my silence, I started to appreciate just how negative my space was and how toxic it had become. I really started dissecting the conversations that I was having with people, and the things that we laughed about, and the things that triggered our phone calls! Why were we calling each other so often? Why did we always feel that we had so much to talk about?

In the 2 to 3 hours that we spent on the phone, what were we talking about? Was it negatively or positively impactful on our lives? Did we speak life into each other? Build each other up or tear each other down? Did we rip apart the fabric that held other individuals together with our spoken words?

I can admit that I've been guilty of focusing on other people's lives and deceived myself that I wasn't playing a judge in their lives, au contraire, I was a third party on the outside merely observing, when in actuality I was doing the sooner, passing judgment! Drawing conclusions from their stories, why they can do certain things that they do, presuming why these individuals could live a lifestyle of their choosing. I had created an entire plot, a concocted fiction as a base for the credo to rationalize why, some may have been right, or wrong; eventually, I realized it was not my place to declare judgment, but to accept them as they were.

In quiet solitude, I've had a lot of time to reflect on myself, and the energy that I exude! I'm a natural observer, I sit back, and I listen to what people say, I observe their actions to see if they harmonize with the words that come out of their mouth. It is essential that our actions conform to our words! In my tranquility, something I discerned was my desire for stability. I desire consistency in the flow of things, with a sound and sensible outcome in any undertaking.

I have evolved into an extreme risk taker. I'm all about being spontaneous and "just going with the flow, "but then again, that only works for me according to my own terms! You must be logical. Otherwise, you fail to come to terms with it all, unless you're okay with silence. When you're busy consuming your life with other people's opinions or putting your dreams and hopes into the hands of others, they then become toxic.

What sometimes happens is we allow others to

pour their energy into our dreams and aspirations. Sometimes we don't see it, but when you "share" your visions and dreams with others, what you don't notice is, the next person is most likely going to spill their energy onto yours. They may not see the vision or picture that you do and may not quite understand the plan; hence, they saturate your positive energy with their negative energy.

You must learn to be okay with your own voice in your tranquil state. You must come to terms with the voice that you hear within, you must be okay with the thoughts that resonate within you. You don't necessarily have to believe every thought that passes through your brain or every emotion that you feel on the inside of you. However, you do have to become one with those things. It is all a part of your system and the way that you flow.

It's why you operate the way that you do, its apart of the reason why you say the things you do, believe the things you do, and do the things that you do! Silence is golden!

It's okay to refrain from the use of social media, ignore phone calls, and purge certain people out of your life and to dissolve toxic and unneeded relationships, or adopt a hiatus if needed.

    I went through a time when I had to hit the pause button on a few relationships and friendships because I needed to take a moment to dissect them because as you navigate through life, you will notice that people are constantly evolving and changing. The person that you may have been yesterday may not be the person that you wake and be today, because change is inevitable. You should always to be open and submissive to change.

    Don't feel less of a person because you decide to take a moment for yourself to be silent. I have always tended to disappear or go missing for a few months at a time with my friendships. You would hear from me in January and February, and by March, I would disappear. At times I would tell my circle don't call me, don't text me, don't look for me, I'm fine. In reality, I just needed a moment to myself. Sometimes it would be from March until July, sometimes August. Whatever length of time I may felt I needed, I used. I've always just reached specific points of my life that I thought I just needed silence.

It's not that I'm necessarily angry or tripping, but sometimes I have so much going on within me. I have such an active mind. The voices and the conversations I have within my own mind tend to get so loud that I can't even stand to take in other people's conversations. Sometimes I feel like I can't tolerate another person's voice. At times, I feel like it would mentally kill me to consume my mind, and life with another person's drama or anger or frustrations.

I have always thought that I must be at a stable place to tolerate a conversation. If you are stressed out and come venting to me, you are going to be upset with my attitude or response, because I am in a mentally delicate position.

Maybe you only need a listening ear, perhaps you just only need some advice or guidance, but I must keep my mental space healthy.

Even in this era with social media, it's like everyone has to know what's going on in everyone's world. Who is dating who? Who went viral and how?

Like everyone is so consumed with each other, and if we just took that exact same energy and put it solely within ourselves, our well -being would be so much healthier! Whether you notice it or not all that energy that you give so freely to others, that's the EXACT same energy that you need to become a better, you! All that love that you sow into others so freely, sow it into yourself!

You know why you continuously feel incomplete or drained? ...Because you just invested in someone else other than yourself!

All that love that you keep giving off is the exact love you are looking for in return, from the person that you are giving it to. However, you want to know why that person won't give it back to you? ...because you don't love you! You don't know what love feels like. You can't identify with it because you are lacking it. You need that conversation with yourself. You need that date with yourself. Until you put yourself first, you will continue to lack.

At what point will you put yourself first? At what point will you love you enough to take care of you before you help anyone else? At what point will you love YOU enough to put YOU first? Sometimes we are out seeking validation in all the wrong places when really; it's within our silence that we are validated. It's within our silence that we come to terms with who we are.

AFRAID OF SILENCE

Silence is scary at times... its gets tricky! It is in my silence that I heard my own loudest cries and pleas. In silence, I started to battle my biggest enemy, which was my own reflection of myself. The thoughts that I had about myself, the way I viewed myself, the way I felt about myself. I had to learn how to check myself in my silence.

In my silence, I got to evaluate EVERYYYYTHING!! I got to dissect the voices that I was hearing within, were they God's voice, was it my own personal heart and emotions speaking to me, am I going CRAZY?!

Let's keep it real!! I had the opportunity to think about my life, happiness and whether I was living in my purpose. Am I doing what I'm supposed to be doing within this thing called "LIFE"? Am I comparing my life to social media or a meme that any one of us could have thought of and created! Am I living through other people"?

Here's a good example: Lisa went to the Bahamas, now I need to go on a trip and outdo Lisa and her baecation, but I have to go borrow somebody else's BAE...OKAY! LOL!! That's a different prayer for a different day with different energy!!

Okay. Jesus, I'm back! However, I got to look at whether I was looking at myself incorrectly. Maybe I was thinking too low of myself and not finding myself worthy of such valuable pedestals in life. I'm personally guilty of having a prior projection of myself, and I've always held myself ... I guess you can say I held myself hostage or accountable to fulfill that idea.

It's so funny because when our prior projectors of ourselves don't look like what God may have lined up in your path, primarily if you don't view yourself as worthy, you may downplay your own greatness! Ever since I was young, and I mean honestly about 8 years old, I remember saying that by the time I was 30 years old that I would be married with 2 or 3 kids, and I was going to beat out that "average American" foolery I heard about retiring at 60. I was going to cut that in half and do that by 30!! Some plan and idea right!! Lol!

Well needless to say I'm 29 years old and I will

be 30 in 5 weeks on June 14th by the grace of God, and not only am I not married, but I'm also not engaged, I'm not in a relationship, I'm not dating! LMAO!!
But......wait for it....

I do have two of the most LIT human beings that God allowed me to birth and entrusted me to navigate, my daughter Xariya and my son Prince-Ariohn.

I'm also not retired. However, I have been blessed to be an entrepreneur, so I don't have to work a 9 to 5. I say that humbly! But you must get rid of this fake concept of who you may portray to be or who you may be inspired by, get down to the core of you and figure out who you are. The more I aligned myself with peace and quiet, becoming one with nature, the more I confided in God, like he was my best friend here on Earth in the physical realm.

The more I sought his face and sincerely tried to get a response from him, look for him exactly where he is, that's when I became more in tune with who I am! That's when I started to understand my worth and my value and put a price on it! That's when I was able to start walking in my purpose! Yet again, none of this took place until I went silent.

I'm a social person, so I get how nerve-wracking that can be most times but again, within that time, I got mentally stronger, my patience increased, my anger lessened, and I grew content. I learned things about me that I never thought I could do. Trust me I've been through those cloudy days!

> *Please don't for a minute believe that
> I wake up to rainbows and unicorns!*

I've had to deal with those gray and dark days too! I've been suicidal! Trust me when I tell you I've been there. However, if I can do something or say something just to save one person's life or just give one-person hope, then I feel like my job is being done correctly! Even if I can only help, someone process their thoughts more clearly or their vision, then I am doing the job.   Even right now at this very moment as I write, I'm sitting in a park in front of Lakeview, alone, just me, God and these words that you are now reading! I mean again like everyone else, I feared what happens or what to expect within it. Of course, we have the apparent aspect of what silence is...hearing nothing!

Many people have never spent time by themselves. Yes, you may be sitting in your house right now alone, but I mean intentionally. Intentionally setting out time in your life to be silent or creating the space to do so.

Silence is finding a safe, quiet place solely meant for you! There are no phones, tablets, no people, no music, NOTHING!! A place, where you can become one with yourself, to focus on you!

Personally, at times I can do this at home, but I also that I feel more open, free when I'm outside with nature, so I spend a lot of my personal time at the beach or parks with bodies of water. I recall an encounter I experienced within my silence that was scary and life changing.

A few years ago, back when I had my own apartment, and it was just my kids and I. During that time, I was a preschool teacher, working over 40 plus hours a week and to me life was just unfair.

Like the old saying goes, "I was getting the doo-doo end of the stick". Over a period, I had grown to be fed up and felt like everyone had me... messed up! I had allowed my circumstances to let me play the victim and suck me into its whirlwind of misery.

On this Friday, as I did many Fridays before this one, my kids were excited and ready to go to their aunt's house for a sleepover. Little do they know I was somewhat considering just disappearing. Yes that means, everything that it could possibly mean. I cuddled and cried with them, kissed them endlessly and told them no matter what don't ever forget I love them!

**INSERT PRAISE BREAK*
OMG JESUSSSSSSSS THANK YOU!!! I'm crying real tears right now, OMMMGGG!!! LORD, YOU ARE REAL!!! YOU ARE WORTHY!!! THANK YOU FOR LOVING ME MORE THAN I COULD EVER LOVE MYSELF!!!!!!

See that praise break is the prelude for what you are about to read. I had dropped the kids off to their aunt's house, and I made my way back home. I went to sit on my patio, which was overlooking a golf course. It was truly a beautiful view. I went into a trance, and was just indulging in my numbness. Then my phone rang, it was my mother! I am not sure if she was lead by the spirit or what to call me, but she did, and boy was she in for it!

I honestly don't remember in detail the words that I said to her, but I do remember rambling about me feeling tired and fed up, and how I felt unappreciated. I rambled for maybe 30 minutes, my poor mom! Our conversation ended along the lines of her telling me that I really needed to consider seeking someone to talk to because she knew how much I would tend to become distant.

For a few more hours, I flirted with the idea of not existing or disappearing. Somewhere along the process I somehow managed to pop, a few slices of pizza in the oven to reheat from the night before, after all, who wants to die hungry right?! LOL! Somehow, I managed to fall asleep on the couch in a matter of minutes. I don't know if it was from the exhaustion of me rambling and crying out to my mom or what exactly took place, but I fell fast asleep. Next thing you know I recall dreaming and saying to myself within it, that

"Something was burning and that you are going to die "a few moments later I physically jumped up out my sleep to my entire apartment being completely covered in some thick fog!

I'm instantly gasping, I'm sweating, I can't see, I'm running to open my doors of the apartment cause literally in the heat of the moment I remember thinking of my neighbors, my kids, and my parents. I'm in complete adrenaline mode taking the pizza out the oven that has burnt to nothing and literally was burning my pan! OMMMGG it was a MESS!!!

Long story short no one was hurt or injured. Thankfully by the grace and mercy of God, but I almost died that night...alone....in my silence. Foolishly of me to desire, just hours before this incident to "disappear," BUT GOD!!!!

See what people fail to realize is that going gray and going dark is such a big area to be within. It's so welcoming to be evil, it's so easy to be upset, miserable and depressed and confused, but YOU DO NOT HAVE TO GO THERE!!!! Even after this whole ordeal, I had to take a moment to be silent afterward.

I didn't accept any phone calls unless you had my kids. I had to take time to get back to a mentally healthy and stable place.

I was lacking stability because I was putting so much of my time, my emotions, my attention, my resources, my energy into others, that I began to lose insight of WHO I am and WHOSE I am. I didn't even put myself divinely here, so who am I to take myself divinely out? Who am I to tell myself how much time I'm supposed to have here or take it away? I didn't create me! Yet every day I should be appreciative of my divine purpose and of my divine creator.

This process didn't happen overnight for me. After my encounter, whenever I felt unsafe or alone, I would purposely go to my parents' home. It's important that you feel safe. That you surround yourself with people that you know genuinely care whether you live or die. Many a time they didn't know why I came around as often as I did, but I knew why, and if it meant saving ME then that's what it's going to be.

I had to get back to the roots of what I know, what I understand, what I can relate to, and the people who try to hear me out with an open heart.

Whatever level you may feel you need to go too within your silence is up to you! Write your thoughts and feelings out, speak them out, and hey, scream them out if you need to! Don't be afraid of what your silence brings you. Again, silence is golden!. Everything that is manifested to you in your silence is golden. Every single thought that you may have in the mist of your silence whether it be negative, positive, hurts, makes you laugh, makes you question stuff, YOU NEED THAT!!!

That's when it's flowing more purely, and you can see and hear it. You don't have negativity within your space telling you what to think, where to go and how to come! It is just what it is, and that another thing find a way to accept and be okay with what it is .Be okay with WHAT IS!!! With what is going on in your life now, the job you do have, the car you do drive, just find an area of contentment. Just be who you are, own who you are. Stand by that. Always remain true to yourself!

SHARING IS NOT ALWAYS CARING!

Be careful with "SHARING"!!! I know, I know, "sharing is caring"!! But sometimes we share our emotions, viewpoints, dreams, and visions with others and most times they cannot see what was placed along your path!

Now they are casting their views onto yours or downplaying your ideas. Or maybe you're feeling some type of way, because they are not as excited as you are about your vision for your life. They cannot see nor picture it for you. It is not up to their standards of thinking about you! That does not mean that your peers hate or that they think too small, it just maybe not intended for them to see or understand. Everybody has their own sole purpose here on this earth, and you may not understand the path that they have decided to tread for themselves either.

Everything that you have been through is a part of your legacy, its apart of your truth, its apart of why you are the way you are or think the way you do or even say the things you do. Love yourself enough to shut everyone out, love yourself enough not to want anyone's opinion, love yourself enough to trust and be confident in how you feel. Love yourself enough to believe in how you think and how you feel. Trust the choices that you make for yourself.

That's the whole point of silence, it's to help you identify which areas need to be worked on, and it enables you to identify those areas that are probably your strong points or your weak points.

It's not until you can put your own life under a microscope and dissect you and can evaluate yourself and be your own worst critic is when you will begin to see progress.

Act like it's the first time you ever had a conversation with yourself, judge yourself, give yourself a rate from 1 to 10 and see where you fall, ask yourself would I date me? Would I carry a conversation with me? Would I start a business with me? If you can't honestly answer those questions or at least be comfortable with your responses, then that should tell you something.

That alone should open the path of reflection and at least give you an idea as to where to start this process. It's not until you can dissect yourself, understand yourself, fix yourself, value yourself, and love yourself, that you will be able to reciprocate that unto others.

A LOVE LETTER TO PAIN

Dear Anxiety,

Today I choose to battle you! I don't remember when we met or how you lured me on. You're so easy for me to read now, yet I fall for you every time. You consume my heart, you send off alerts in my brain, you send my heart on this emotional rollercoaster, you take away my ability to feel in control, instead, you smother me. You often astound me and increase my discomfort. The closer you get to catching me the more intense this process gets. I'm now telling myself when exactly to gasp for air, my body feels like it's been set ablaze, sweat is now raining through my pores. When will this screaming be silenced? Oh Lord, I told you, I cannot do this anymore.

Remember it's Not Personal, it's Purpose!

ROMANS 8: 30-31

Those who God decided in advance would be conformed to his son, he also called. Those whom he called, he also made righteous. Those whom he made righteous, he also glorified. So, what are we going to say about these things? If God is for us, who is against us?

THE CALLING

"You are a square peg, trying to fit into a round hole"- my Dad

One thing about being called is that it's not just one big moment in your life that you get this urge to be different. The calling happens at multiple phases and stages of your life. I can recall when I was about maybe 9 or 10 years old and being at church on a Sunday, it was basically the ending part of service where people usually dedicate their lives to God. I don't recall the sermon topic but what did stand out was this interesting moment. Bishop Henry Fernandez is praying and asking if anyone was interested, and if so to come down to the front of the church. As I stood at my seat, eyes closed, the spiritual strings of my heart were being tugged on, by God. I heard a voice of someone saying, "you need to go down to the altar". I instantly opened my eyes and looked beside me but, everyone was caught in the moment. Once again, I tightly clenched my eyelids shut as if I heard nothing. However, I heard that voice again "YES!! I'm talking to you, GO!" At this point, my heart is ready to jump out of my chest, and a sense of a heat wave consumes my body. I'm fighting with myself and stumbling over my own nerves, alter call is maybe about three to five minutes, and I am stressing myself out about whether I should go down to the front or not. I do recall my dad releasing my hand because obviously, the spirit had moved him to go down for his own reasons. Now, I'm really shaken! I'm still debating inside my head whether I'm tripping and hearing voices or what's what! LOL

    Bishop is looking around the congregation, and he said, "there's someone who is wrestling with what they are hearing and what they should do" and how he would extend the altar call for an additional two minutes. Filled with fear, adrenaline, and confusion, a voice within yelled "GOOOO!!!" one last time and I instantly shoot down to the front of the church, squeezed a spot in next to my dad, grabbed his hand, and clenched my eyelids so tightly.

    I didn't know what I was doing, what I was hearing, or what was next! I just did what I felt I was supposed to do! I mean, I was scared out my boots! LOL! This is one of the first real moments that I remember not really understanding what exactly it was or meant from this day forth. After this incident, NOTHING CHANGED! I went back to my usual routine of being a kid, nothing supernatural or abnormal took place.

When I was younger, I remember battling with self-identity and always trying to figure out where exactly it was that I belonged. I remember a time in middle school when all my friends and associates were the opposite of me. The girls were sexually active, dating, and then there was me. I couldn't have a boyfriend; I couldn't date as my parents did, adopting the traditional church upbringing.

Everything the average middle and high school student had or was doing.. that was not me.

The house parties, senior skip days (even though I did, and they never knew once a month and twice once I started feeling myself......HEYYY GEORGE AND BEV!!) lol! Harry Potter, cell phones, Jordan's! NO, they were not doing that. Don't get it twisted, my parents worked their butts off and made sure I had everything I needed and pretty much everything I wanted. I always felt that I stood out and that I was different from the crowd that I hung around. I use to feel invisible because I felt that everything that I was never enough.

I was always cool with the "IT CROWD," and I guess you can say that I was somewhat apart of it because I associated with them; however, I was never doing what they were. It is not that I didn't want to, or that I believe I was superior to anyone else. However, I was just scared of my parents. LOL!! That's the truth!!

I remember I use to feel invisible because I felt that everything that I was not enough. That it didn't hold value because it wasn't "POPULAR" or what the "IT CROWD" represented. I even recall back in high school going into 11th grade and 12th grade, it seemed like everyone was starting to or had already discovered who they were.

My circle of people all knew what college they were going to attend, what their major was, when they would graduate, what sorority or fraternity they were going to pledge, what job or hustle they would have to make money, who they would come home with on holidays.

I was surrounded by some real movers and shakers! I remember we use to take the career path tests that would ask you a host of questions, and its purpose was to help direct or steer you down a path of your interests. My results were always even across the board. I was always the person who felt neutral about things in life. Nothing stood out more than the other.

Everyone just seemed to have it all together. Once again, I had no plans! I had no idea who I was, or where I wanted to be. By my mid-senior year, I still had not filled out one college application because not only did I not have interest in attending, I didn't know what I would even be going for! I remember graduation happening, and I'm going around helping others pack up for school, and that's when it hit me!

Umm...hello.... earth to Shay, what's your next move? There's a missing piece to your puzzle, what is it?"

I remember confiding in my family trying to seek clarity and direction as to what my next steps should be. After all this is my family and they care for me, they should be able to look at me and define me. They should be able to look at me and identify my purpose and my calling. My whole life my family has validated me and orchestrated my life, so now what?!

So, they did what they felt was best and pointed me in the direction of nursing; so, I enrolled, I completed about 2 semesters, and I concluded that it wasn't for me. So fast forward, I quit school and picked up a 9 to 5, and the pay was pretty good, considering my predicament at the time. Once again, I'm influenced by my environment.

I'm a victim of what I see, which is MONEY, and now someone else's dream that has come to pass is now mine!

Now I'm back in school for pharmacy, from there, medical assisting, fashion, to barbering! LOL! I was trying to figure out who I was! Oh and as for jobs, we're not even going to touch on that subject! Fast forward some years later, and social media is really LIT! Its graduation season and now my classmates are receiving associates, bachelors, masters, and higher degrees, and here I am, yet and still, at square one!

Now I have the urge to graduate with just about any degree, just because I am influenced by my environment. Here I was making good money and not knowing what to do with it because I was too caught up on what other people had going on. Now I'm trying to make sure I'm up to date with fashion, music, what's trending, the best quote, just getting more and more lost in who I was NOT!

See in your calling, you notice that you think differently. Your thoughts are elevated! You crave more! You create uniquely!

The calling is that thought when you wake up and say to yourself "NO! This can't be my life" like you truly don't accept your circumstances. YES, we must deal with them, but you can decide to figure out a plan out of that issue. The calling is like this longing feeling to belong, but you don't ever know WHO it is that you are looking for or WHAT it is that you are looking for, but it's this constant desire to find it!! To discover it!!

To comfort that longing! I remember feeling like I had to dig a little deeper into who I am... and soul search because this cannot be it! Deep within me, I have always felt that I was more significant and made for more than what I was doing, so I had to go find that thing!! Here's an idea of how the calling works,

Imagine you're in a mall and you hear someone call your name out in the crowd. You stop in your tracks and start looking all around, but you don't recognize any of the faces that are in your line of vision. So, you continue to go on about your business, but someone calls out your name again. Once again, you can't see them, but obviously, it's someone who sees and knows you! Because you can't see them, you now must rely on your senses. The person calls out your name another two times, and you focus in on what direction their voice is coming from.

As you use your ability to discern, you navigate your way through the crowd until the voice gets louder and louder and more precise to hear. Like an old game of Marco Polo! It's not until you become face to face with that person that you will be able to identify who it is and where the location is. The calling is very similar!

The more you walk the path, and the more in tune you get with yourself, the easier it will be for you to identify your value, your identity, your purpose, your calling!

The calling can be stressful, annoying, nerve-wrecking and overwhelming at times because you're always trying to get it right! After the battling with whether you are crazy or not, hearing voices or maybe being shown visions, you start to work and align your life with what you see. The problem tends to come into play when what we see and what's taking place currently in our reality isn't matching up. See that's just it, your viewpoint is wrong! All of it IS your reality.

All of it IS exactly how it's going to happen for you! Though your current situation may not be the ultimate bigger picture that you see in your mind, it IS still a reference point! It shows you exactly where you are now in your journey. You may be seeing the finished product, maybe it's just a mid-way point! Whatever it is, it's on YOU to determine what the next steps are in between where you are and where you ultimately see yourself

THE GIFT

So, I come across Steve Harvey's "The Gift" and let's just say he has opened my perception in more ways than one! To summarize what he spoke on,

...everyone has a God-given gift and it's something that comes naturally to you! You don't necessarily have to go to school for it because it was given to you at creation and you were born with it.

Well me? I struggled with what "MY GIFT" was. I can't sing, I'm not athletic; I'm not a dancer, what is my gift? What can I do without thinking about it? The calling helped me to identify what my gift and purpose are, and now I can walk in alignment. But this all starts with you first being silent. After you've become one with being silent, dissect yourself, and you will begin to highlight areas of interest, creativity, talents, and gifts!

Once you have a clearer understanding of your gift, you must dissect that as well! You want to make sure that you're using your gift properly. Your gift is bigger than you! Your gift is about others; so, you want to make sure that it's not being used in vain, and that my friend is when you begin to align your life with your calling and can begin to walk in purpose. Your gift WILL make room for you! Your gift will give you clarity! Your path will start to open for you and opportunity will now come pursuing you, because you are pursuing it!

The calling provides clarity along your journey. It almost shines a light into those dark and gray areas and directs you on to the next step! When you begin to acknowledge the fact that you are called, you start evaluating everyone and everything around you. The fact that I now have a clear understanding and I can see what my next step should be, it makes me want to wipe out anything that may slow me down or get in my way.

After going through life with no sense of direction and running into dead ends, I finally know what to do. The calling comes off as reassuring. One thing about God, wherever he guides, he provides!!! And he backs up all his plans for you with constant confirmation.

The calling aligned me with my gift!

Though I've been using my gift unknowingly, it wasn't until I started to get aligned with the calling that I figured out which path is mine to own. Every job that I've worked, everyone who turned their back on me, every broken heart, every frustrating day, every tear I have screamed and cried, every time I wanted to die, was all well designed to push me to this moment!

Everyone has a purpose and a job to get done here on earth. Dissect your struggle, figure out your pain, figure out what went wrong, and determine what it is that you had to learn.

Obstacles come into your life to teach you and redirect you! Every time you were told no, it stirred up something on the inside of you! Every time you didn't get the job or the opportunity, it stirred up something inside of you! Your friend stole your business idea and is now profiting from it, and that stirred up something inside of you! That relationship that failed, that friendship that ended, now you feel all anxious and worked up like you need to make a change, that overwhelming feeling, that feeling of being anxious and flustered, that's God, calling you!

That's his way of showing you what's going wrong in your life. That's his way of getting your attention! It's up to you to determine how strong of a test and how long of a test he allows.

The calling will go to whatever extent it needs to, just to get to you; until you reach a certain level in life and are ready to make the necessary changes to becoming a better and more aligned you!

Remember it's Not Personal, it's Purpose!

PSALMS 25:8-12

The Lord is good and does the right thing; he teaches sinners which way they should go. God guides the weak to justice, teaching them his way. All the Lord's paths are loving and faithful for those who keep his covenant and laws. Where are the ones who honor the Lord? God will teach them what path to take.

IDENTIFYING MY GIFT

Again, I don't sing, dance, I'm not athletic, I can't draw so I had difficulty identifying my gift. When I focused in on me and really took my skills and talents apart, the only thing that I came to as my conclusion, that I can do effortlessly, at any given time, was TALK! LOL! Can you believe that?

I mean I really dug deep into my life, and one thing that I always got in trouble for in every school, from elementary to high school, was always talking and laughing! High school I got kicked out of numerous of classes. It got so bad that my 10th grade English teacher, Mrs. Stanbrook, banned me from her class for the remainder of the year, so I spent a lot of my time 'assisting' other teachers. LOL!
Whenever I wanted to tell someone something, my stories would always come out long and drawn out. Like I would give you every ingredient and measurement to the TEA! LOL! I've counseled friendships, and weirdly enough, marriages!

This same talking that drove everyone crazy growing up is the same voice that saved two of my closest friends from committing suicide at two different times in my life!

It was my words that have inspired and motivated others to get married, to start a business, to pursue a degree; and God knows I say this humbly! When you're going through the motions, you don't see the impact that you may be having on someone. It's not until times like now, when I'm in alignment and have become in tune with who I am. Now recognizing my purpose and seeing that God was using me then and had me moving in purpose.

Growing up, I use to enjoy writing, maybe because I couldn't adequately express my thoughts without being interrupted or rushed. I used to write skits, poems, movies, short stories, you name it. But somewhere growing up these things lessened, and it was more than likely my environment.

You lose sight at times, on what makes you happy or content because you start adjusting your ideas or

plans because they (your entourage) are not on the bandwagon.

So, you find yourself picking up bad qualities like adjusting and changing to what others want to do, or what they like or what they feel is "popular"! Now you're getting further and further away from whom you are and what's important to you, which usually leads you to the place of uncertainty and being confused and lost as to who you are and what you were created for.

TIRED OF CRYING

I'm so tired of crying, it's like a chainsaw is continuously cutting through to my heart. Here it comes again… damn these voices that are being screamed from my soul, this feeling is making me lose control. Heart racing, adrenaline pumping, the lion is roaring, my thoughts are soaring; Here goes the warm puddles again! Been spending my time searching within, but this one here, I can't quite comprehend. Am I breathing? This has got to change! Drowning in over thinking or 'under thinking'; I just wish I could stop thinking, instead. Confined to my bed, lost in prayer, please Lord if you dare, rescue me because I'd rather be dead instead, I'm so tired of crying….

Remember it's Not Personal, it's Purpose!

JAMES 1:2-4

My brothers and sisters, please think of the various tests you encounter as occasions for joy. After all, you know that the testing of your faith produces endurance. Let this endurance complete its work so that you may be fully mature, complete and lacking in nothing.

TRUST THE PROCESS

What the heck does this saying really mean? You want to know a good way to piss me off, just tell me to trust the process! LOL! That's the exact thing that I have an issue with, is the process! I don't understand everything that is taking place within it!

How long is this process? Is this process even worth it? I mean, I've gotten this far, right?! I don't see the whole picture within the process.

Everything that I once knew and grew to be comfortable with is changing. My entire world may be flipped upside down, and I can't see past today. I'm expected to trust the process that I can't share with anyone. Trust the process, when my family thinks I'm crazy for saying I believe I'm called! Trust the process, when I had to bury 12 of my own family members in 1 year! Trust the process, when the whole world has turned their backs on me.

Trust the process, when I've been watching other people try to trust their process, and they end up breaking in the process, or maybe they have been processing for an extended amount of time, and you don't see their dreams or hearts desires being manifested.

How do I trust the process when I have not seen anyone that makes it through the process? Or, no one to guide me down the path. For you to properly trust the process, I feel like it starts in your mind. You got to have a healthy foundation. Do not become a prisoner of your own brain. You must be able to see more; you have to be able to create you a way out of your situation. and not just random acts. Your gift, your calling, your purpose, your journey! That will make room for you!

It's your lane to claim and own because it's your path that you're traveling along and it's your purpose that you are pursuing. You reach a point within the process that after some affirmations here and there we continue along the journey with confidence. God will give you constant affirmation and confirmation that you are indeed NOT losing your mind and you are moving in alignment with your purpose.

Be a person of your words, of your thoughts, of your prayers. You just make sure that you get into alignment and stay in alignment. Walk your path. Do not ever feel as if the next person's life is better than yours or that they are more blessed. Realize that everyone deals with their own set of problems.

The more time you spend on trying to time the process and figure it all out, the more time that is being lost. Trusting the process is about believing that "all things are working together for my good." Your process doesn't really make sense to you until way after the fact. Every job, friendship, relationship, failed opportunity, every promotion, every idea, it ALL comes together.

As you begin to walk along your journey, you will notice when all the foolishness has paid off.

Since I have started walking in purpose, it now makes sense to me how I ended up working at Walgreens and job-hopping all over. I see why certain people tested me at jobs, why certain friendships had to end, why relationships were torn apart; I understand that God did not allow me to confide in anyone much growing up. I see how deciding nursing wasn't for me awakened my thoughts and pushed me into other directions. I understand why God closed some doors and why he opened others.

Trusting the process is when things are not going in your favor or moving according to your time frame, but you keep on holding on. It is when you want to quit the job, but keep showing up. Trusting the process all comes down to having some hope and faith. Trusting the process is about believing for better, even though your circumstances are showing you otherwise.

It is finding that little flicker of hope, can one day catch a flame! You must have a little bit of fight buried deep down inside of you! YOU ARE WORTH IT! You deserve to be able to rest peacefully at night and not just sleep!

***You deserve to laugh, to smile, to have confidence, to have dignity, to have peace! You deserve to be free, and you can be, and you will be when you walk the walk!* Notice I said walk and not talk!**

Everyone deals with things differently, and choose to share whatever they please and however, they wish! A LOT of people will look like they are on top of the world and living their best lives if all they are showing are their wins! Listen to me when I tell you, trust the process!! You just never know how amazing you are or may become!

You never know who you are going to meet at any given time that may possibly change your life forever! Think of trusting the process as a relationship gone badly. You're in this relationship, you get cheated on, lied to and taken for granted. You must separate yourself from that person and, take some time to heal and re-cooperate. One thing I can assure you, is if you don't fight back for you then why should or would anyone else? Besides, can you really blame them?

Some time goes by, and now you are longing for a relationship again and feel that you are ready to give a new person a shot at your heart, however, because of your previous heartbreak, now you're a little more reserved. Now you're going into the situation a little more cautious. Just because you had one bad experience, it should not deter you from what is set out for you!

Just because the last person hurt you, does not mean the next person will do the same. You must rebuild your hope within people, and your patience! When that new person comes along and wows you and catches you by surprise, you're going to want to go into this new situation with new hope, new peace, and a new type of patience! You can't go along with carrying burdens.

Trusting the process is when things are not going in your favor or moving according to your time frame.

But you keep on keeping on it's when you want to quit the job, but you show up faithfully because you know you got kids and bills. It's when business flops, or the marriage fails, that you know at that very moment, whatever situation that you may be facing right now, it will not break you! I didn't say it wouldn't hurt, or it's not going to suck, because it is, and it will. BUT you will overcome that!

Fight back for your independence, fight back for your love, fight back for your career, fight back for your business, fight back for your purpose and your calling, fight back for YOU! One thing I can assure you is if YOU don't fight than anybody else in this world will!

Can you blame them? Why should they? Do it for you! Love yourself enough to save you, value yourself enough! I assure you that there is purpose upon your life and it's solely up to you to answer that calling!

Think of trusting the process as, using a GPS.

Let's say you're going on a road trip to Georgia and you've never been before. You've used your GPS numerous times for local destinations, but now you're going to be using new routes and highways. You input your current location and the address to your destination. Sarah (the GPS lady! LOL) is giving you direction by direction onto the highway. Once you've reached, she lets you know that you may be about 300 miles or so away from your destination and what time you should arrive.

For about the first 2 hours of the trip, you're happy-go-lucky, singing tunes, eating snacks, enjoying the scenery. You feel content and comfortable. Now the sun is starting to go down, but you still can see pretty well, you're still comfortable and content. Now it's about 9:30pm and its dark out, but there are lots of streetlights, so you're still riding in confidence and contentment. You would prefer daylight out, but hey!

About 10:30pm, the street lights are starting to decrease, and now you're feeling a little "iffy" you're checking your phone to make sure the GPS didn't turn off or that it's not on mute! Sarah had a lot to say at the beginning of this journey, but now she's quiet; Now it's 10:50pm and its pitch black on the road. The only lights you see are from the cars that may pass you by. You're starting to kind of panic because this is unfamiliar turf, you're alone, and Sarah's quiet and even though you're looking at the destination on your phone telling you which direction to go, even when Sarah is quiet!

Just because you're starting to build up anxiety and your feeling unsafe, does not mean you're going to stop and pull over alongside the road! I mean, yeah you can do that, that is an option, but then you will be practically stranded, in the same pitch black until the sun comes back up! But you're not going to do that! You're going to continue to push through that anxiety or nervousness.

You're going to try and find distractions to keep you uplifted and in a positive mood. You make some adjustments along the way to make you more comfortable or to make your journey more manageable. You may kick your shoes off, open the window for a bit to catch some fresh air, switch up the music your listening to, you know, just whatever you feel necessary to get to where you are going.

Even though Sarah hasn't given you an update, she's always watching to make sure you are going in the correct direction, keeping you in alignment with the destination. You know this because at any time you take a detour off that path, for example, if you pull over at a rest stop; Sarah will then show up and speak a word to you and tell you how to get back on the right path. She speaks when you need redirecting. It's not until you begin to see signs that say "welcome to Georgia" that you know you are near your destination.

At this point, you're confident and content again, because now you have been given some affirmation that you are going down the right path, but you had to trust Sarah's long silent moment because she knows your destination and has given you direction. It's up to you to push through and continue to drive despite how uneasy you were feeling.

It was either push through or quit and stops mid-way and pick up later or just completely turn around and just go back home and not go to Georgia.

It's not until you reach that exact address, that you feel the most at peace and happy because not only has

Sarah started talking again, but her last words to you were "You have arrived." You see that it was all worth it in the end! It all worked together for your good!

The anxiety, the nervousness, the fresh air, switching my music, taking off my shoes, all of it came together at the end of the journey and helped me to reach my destination.

Trusting the process is just that, a process! But no matter what obstacles, setbacks, bad decisions, whatever comes your way, just know, it all has a purpose, and it's a part of your journey! TRUST THE PROCESS!

Remember it's Not Personal, it's Purpose!

PSALMS 32:8

I will instruct you and teach you about the direction you should go. I'll advise you and keep my eye on you.

BREATHE

Today I encourage you to plan a day for yourself just to breathe! Don't make any plans, just chill out for the day whether it may be at home, at the beach, the park, take a mini vacation if you can. Just take a day to focus on your blessings that are happening in your life. The fact that you are still breathing is the greatest blessing of them all! That means you have another chance to start over, another chance to figure it out, another opportunity to try harder, push harder, another chance to do it right. It's another chance for you to create a new opportunity.

When you have arrived at this point in your journey, it starts to become very clear to you, WHO you are and WHOSE you are! You begin to question anyone or anything that may be trying to come along your path. Now you're not interested in doing certain things, your perspective may have changed, you have made some decisions, you are evolving! If there's anything that does not agree with your choices, lifestyle, or way of thinking, then you cut it short, or you cut it off!

You don't have time to waste anymore! All

along, you just wanted to know how to get to the destination, now you know. Do what you must do!

Take all the necessary steps to assure that you reach your destination. I assure you the path will be long, rigorous, crucial, and heartbreaking at times and lonely ALL of the time, but it's necessary! You want to find out who you really are? What you are fully capable of? Just focus on your journey, you will get there. I beg of you, just take a moment to breathe. After all, it is not personal, it is purpose.

I know you're questioning your life, I understand your circumstances are unfair, I know you feel drained, and all cried out, I know you feel suicidal, but please, I beg of you, just take a moment to just...
BREATHE.

Remember it's Not Personal, it's Purpose!

JEREMIAH 29:11

I know the plans I have in mind for you, declares the Lord; they are plans for peace, not disaster, to give you a future filled with hope.

Remember it's Not Personal, it's Purpose!

PRAYER

"May the Lord bless you and protect you. May he make his face shine down on you and be gracious onto you. May the Lord lift up his face to you and grant you peace."-Numbers 6: 24-26

In Jesus Name,

Amen

Made in the USA
Columbia, SC
27 June 2025